10 Things I Learned When My Husband Had a Girlfriend

by

KATRINA OLIVER THOMAS

I appreciate your support Dawn! Thank you! Katrina

This is a work of fiction, and names, characters, places, and incidents are strictly the product of the author's imagination. Any and all resemblance to actual persons, living or dead, events, or locales is entirely coincidental.

Copyright © 2021 Katrina Oliver Thomas

All rights reserved. No part of this publication may be reproduced, stored in or introduced into a retrieval system, or transmitted, in any form, or by any means (electronic, mechanical, photocopying, recording, or otherwise), without the prior written permission of both the copyright owner and the above publisher of this book.

Acknowledgments

This book has been over ten years in the making. It has been an exciting, and at times, terrifying journey. To paraphrase Habakkuk: 2-3: *write your vision plainly so that when you read it, you can run with and manifest it; it might take a minute, but it will happen.* With that scripture ringing in my head, I created a five-year vision board back in 2018. One of my goals listed on that board was to become a published author—I accomplished that goal in three years.

Getting to this point wasn't easy. There were times when I wanted to abandon my mission. Thankfully, God put some people in my life who held me accountable for making sure this goal was manifested. I want to take a moment and thank those people:

My children (Madison, Myles, and B.J.)—y'all encouraged me when I couldn't encourage myself. I love y'all more than you know.

My friends (Nola Grant and Teress 'Neekie' Truss)—the two of you cared about this book as much as I did. I appreciate y'all more than you know. Thank you! Thank you! Thank you!

My Beta Readers (Shannan Harper and Brittney Urquhart) for their honest feedback. It was crucial to the success of the book. Thank you.

A special shout out to Best-selling Author, Brian W. Smith, for taking the time to answer the many questions I had and for the brotherly advice. I appreciate you.

Lastly, I want to thank the readers for your support. I hope the lessons I've learned help you to better understand your situation and allow you to see that you are not alone.

Although things may seem hopeless at times, with God's Word you will get through it, heal, and move on with your life.

~ Katrina Oliver Thomas

Prologue

My husband had a girlfriend. I'm not talking about some woman he worked with who happened to be a girl. Not a woman whose family was so close to his when they were kids that they were raised like cousins. I'm not even talking about that annoying "friendly" neighbor who happens to be single, curvaceous, and is always in need of a little *muscle* to help her fix something at her house. Nope, I'm not referring to any of those plausible scenarios. When I say my husband had a girlfriend, I'm talking about a: go out on dates, take her kids to school, text when he wakes up and at night before he goes to sleep…girlfriend.

Needless to say, I was devastated when I found out. That's not hyperbole. I'm not exercising creative licensing when I write this. When I use the word "devastated" to describe how I felt at that time, I mean it in every sense of the word. I was depressed—the type that makes you avoid bathing for days and keeps you tethered to your bed. Thoughts of suicide flooded my mind to the point that I found myself waking in the middle of the night and gasping for air like a person who is drowning. To make matters worse, while I laid in my bed staring at the ceiling in a room that reeked of my unwashed armpits, the only thing that seemed to stop my crying were thoughts of murdering my husband and his girlfriend. Murderous thoughts, like the kind chronicled on the television show *Forensic Files*, flooded my mind. Yes...it was that serious.

Fortunately for me—and my cheating husband—I am a God-fearing woman. It was God's grace that ultimately brought me out of what was the darkest period in my life. Once I turned the entire situation over to God, something remarkable happened. The fog lifted. My eyes opened. The desire to wallow in my pain dissipated. Thoughts that were once shrouded in anger and resentment cleared up enough for me to see the lesson in all that I was going through.

Despite the pain I had to endure because of my husband's and another woman's selfish actions, I was able to dry my tears long enough to identify the teachable moments embedded in the situation. The things I learned will help me be a better mate—and choose a better mate—in the future. My hope is that when you finish this book you will feel enlightened and empowered to deal with potential red flags in your own relationships.

Chapter 1

I Had Death on My Mind

Hurt people...*hurt* people. In my case, not only did I want to hurt them, I gave serious thought to hurting myself—humiliation will do that to you. I realize I'm not the first man or woman to be cheated on, and I will not be the last. It's estimated that fifty percent of all marriages end in divorce. Of that fifty percent, infidelity is still the leading cause but that fact didn't make it any less painful. Sprinkle the statistics with a lifestyle that seemed to be rooted in Godly principles, and my husband's behavior was not only puzzling, it caught me completely off guard.

My husband and I are ordained ministers. We were married twenty-five years and have three beautiful children. Picturesque would best describe the life we lived. Unfortunately, things aren't always what they appear to be. My husband, the man who always had a strong opinion of how other folks lived their lives, performed a one hundred-eighty-degree turn—regarding his "taste" in women—that still makes my head spin when I think about it.

Sigmund Freud once said, "The more perfect a person is on the outside, the more demons they have on the inside." I learned of this quote after my marriage; had I known of it during my marriage my reaction to my husband's affair might have been different.

In hindsight, I wonder if I was more hurt by the affair or that he chose to cheat with a woman who—at least on paper—couldn't hold a candle to me. Is that ego talking? Maybe. But I think it's safe to say that it's only natural to hope that the person your spouse cheats on you with is spiritually, physically, emotionally, and/or financially better than you—or all the above. Anything less than that is the equivalent of pouring salt into an open wound. When I look at the person whom he cheated with, what my husband did to me was the equivalent of pouring a bag of salt into a compound fracture.

When I reflect on that period of life, I get mad at myself because the signs of his infidelity were there. The first—and most glaring sign—was that his routine changed. He went from getting home at roughly the same time every evening to often having to work late. The second sign was when I'd call him to inquire about his whereabouts, he'd often let my call go to voicemail and then reply moments later with a text message. There were other signs, but I don't think I need to list them all. I'm sure you've read them before in other books or heard them from your friends or may have experienced the same deceit. What's most important to mention is how my naivety made me feel once I reflected on everything. Quite frankly, I felt like a fool. Those feelings of inadequacy led me to transitioning from wanting to hurt my husband and his girlfriend, to considering doing the unthinkable—committing suicide.

The suicidal thoughts that danced in my head weren't fleeting. They weren't like a drifter who passes through town and stops at the local diner for a sip of coffee and slice of pie before moving along. These thoughts took up permanent residence in my head, and no matter how hard I tried to evict them, they stubbornly remained like an opportunistic squatter. I considered overdosing on prescription medication while wearing an outfit he said he liked, and leaving a suicide note addressed to him. Or, intentionally driving off the road and crashing into something at a place that only he would know the sentimental value. I was uncertain of the method I'd use, but I was seriously considering killing myself in a way that would shackle him with enough guilt to make moving on impossible. But there was one problem—if I killed myself just to get back at him, who would take care of my children?

Once I realized that hurting myself was the ultimate exercise in futility, I was forced to turn to God—my rock—and find a way to not only deal with the anger in me, but rid myself of the guilt I felt for not being able to keep my husband from cheating. It was through prayer and meditation that I learned some things that could not only benefit me moving forward, but could possibly help others going through the same ordeal. Notice I said "others" because I realize that being cheated on is not something that only happens to women; there are a lot of men who have dealt with the same betrayal. So, the lessons I espouse in this book are for anyone to embrace and learn from.

Through prayer, I was able to refocus on the things in my life that mattered the most. Quiet time is what I needed. Time that would allow me to speak to God and hear the instructions He had for me. Without God's word serving as the foundation of any decision I made, I knew that I would miss the lessons that I was supposed to take away from my experiences.

Please keep reading this book so that you can see the ten lessons that I learned:

Lesson: 1 ~ Vengeance Is Not Mine

All things work together for my good. While I was going through my marital problems, I couldn't see how my struggles were working for my good, but I wasn't going to stop believing that the situation would somehow make me a better person. I also realized that as much as I wanted to hurt them both, and trust me I wanted to, it was not my place to make either of them pay for their choices. Instead of taking matters into my own hands, I prayed and journaled. Not every thought I expressed in my journal was holy and pure. I wrote a few cuss words on those pages. But one thing I learned about myself during that time was that I could not take up residency in a place of anger and hate. Forgiveness was a choice that had to be made. Through prayer and journaling I was able to realize these points:

- Neither murder nor suicide was the answer to the hurt, pain, and betrayal I felt. Truth be told, suicide is a selfish act, and the stain of being labeled a murderer would be attached to my children just as much as it would be attached to my legacy.
- The best thing I could do for myself was to use the pain that was meant to break me (and nearly did) to become a better me.
- How I process my pain and anger will be the real testament to who I am as a person.
- Our children should not have to carry the burden of explaining our wrongdoings. Nor, should they have to walk around wondering if the emotions that drove us to make wrong decisions have been passed down to them via genetics.
- My life is valuable and so am I. Rather than viewing the loss of my marriage—due to my spouses'

actions—as a loss, view it as a blessing in disguise. In order to make way for the new, the old must be purged.

Here are some scriptures that helped me deal with the desire to commit suicide and get payback on my husband:

- Romans 12:17-19 states, "Do not repay anyone evil for evil. Be careful to do what is right in the eyes of everyone. If it is possible, as far as it depends on you, live at peace with everyone.
- Do not take revenge, my dear friends, but leave room for God's wrath, for it is written: "It is mine to avenge; I will repay," says the Lord."
- Deuteronomy 32:35 states, "Vengeance is Mine, and retribution, in due time their foot will slip; for the day of their calamity is near, and the impending things are hastening upon them."
- 1 Peter 5:7 states, "Cast all your anxiety on him because he cares for you."

Chapter 2

What's in the Dark Will Come to Light

If I had a dime for every time I wondered what my husband's girlfriend had over me that would make him choose her, I would be a multi-millionaire by now. Before learning of their relationship, I'd never suffered from low self-esteem. I always felt I was attractive. That feeling was confirmed by the flirtatious stares and remarks I'd hear from other men. I always felt successful—the degrees and income I earned were proof of that. I was always faithful—my twenty-year track record of avoiding situations that could even remotely appear "questionable" was proof of that. I was a good mother—my kids have been my biggest supporters and have turned out to be respectful and productive citizens. Lastly, I was willing to be a wife in every sense of the word to him. Yet, he still went out and got a *girlfriend*.

It took a while for me to get it through my thick head that my husband's decision to cheat had nothing to do with me. That was a *him* issue, not a *me* issue.

There are millions of articles, books, and theories out there that tackle the topic of why people have extra-marital affairs. I'm not here to dispute and/or disprove any of the rationalities that have been offered. The only point I want to make in this book—because it's the only point that matters to the person who has been cheated on—is that it is **not your fault**. You can't control the actions of your spouse no more than the weatherman can control the weather. Much like the weatherman can try to predict the weather, you can only evaluate your spouses' actions and words and try to predict how he/she will act when you're not around.

Even if you are astute enough to spot the signs and can predict that your spouse is cheating, it doesn't lessen the sting. Even as I tell my story, the memories remind me of just how far I have come on my journey of forgiveness. I no longer get riled up and become a motor-mouth when describing what happened. As a matter of fact, now would be as good a time as any to take you back to the day I found out about my husband's girlfriend.

Throughout our marriage, my husband would always make disparaging remarks about women who lacked a formal education, lived in poverty, and struggled to establish a *respectable* career. Comments like "ghetto" and "alley ratchet *hoes*" were his go-to insults whenever the topic of one of *those* kinds of women came up. Imagine my surprise when I learned that he cheated on me with a woman who checked every stereotypical box he proclaimed to despise. His girlfriend had five kids by four men; had nothing more than a high school education; was unemployed and relied on the child support checks from her "baby-daddy's" to live; cursed like a sailor; and by his own admission, loved to fight. A Pulitzer Prize winning writer couldn't have created a woman more opposite than me.

Here is the definition of the word *secret*: done, made, or conducted without the knowledge of others. What the dictionary fails to state is that at some point all secrets are revealed. The way my husband's dirty little secret was revealed is proof that when God feels it's time for you to know the truth about a situation, it will be revealed.

My husband and I used the same computer. One day, I checked my emails. When I turned on the computer, his email account was open; he forgot to log out. This wasn't uncommon, he'd forgotten to log out before. When it happened, I would just log out of his account and then open my account. On this day, when I started to close his account, I noticed an unopened email. It was easy to spot because it was bold—the other emails weren't.

Believe me when I say, I'm not a snoop. But, when you see a subject line in your spouses' email that says: *Thank You for Staying with Us,* and you know you haven't been with him to any hotels, your instincts take over. The voice telling you to peek, drowns out the voice telling you to mind your business. Getting to the bottom of the matter becomes your primary focus.

I hesitated as I was about to open the email because I knew my worst fear was about to be confirmed, but my

10 Things I Learned When My Husband Had a Girlfriend!

curiosity won out. I grabbed the mouse, moved the cursor over the email, and clicked.

The email was sent from Super 8 motel. I could feel one of my eyebrows curve like the McDonald's arches. I'm sure I looked like the movie star, The Rock, when he makes one of his eyebrows raise. My mind raced. Questions flashed across my mind like ads on a billboard in downtown Manhattan. When did either of us stay at a Super 8 motel? What would make either of us select a Super 8 motel to stay in? Could this email have been mistakenly sent? When the answer to my questions kept coming back, *no*, my female intuition kicked into overdrive.

The date of his stay at the motel was during the time my kids and I were in Birmingham, Alabama, visiting relatives. I remembered that he was unreachable during that weekend I, but I didn't assume he was doing anything wrong. As it turns out, he was doing a lot of things wrong. Then I thought about something my grandma taught me: *'What's done in the dark always comes to the light.'*

The very next day, I received an anonymous letter in the mail telling me to ask my husband about the woman he was dating. The sender of the letter even gave me his girlfriend's phone number. Within a twenty-four-hour period, the darkness where my husband hid his girlfriend was luminated light the skies at a 4th of July fireworks display. Here is the second lesson I learned:

Lesson: 2 ~ It's a Him Issue, not a You Issue

Stop beating yourself up. Are you perfect? No. Don't spend time trying to figure out what you did wrong because even if you were the worst mate who ever walked the face of the earth, the decision to have an extra-marital affair is the responsibility of the person who did the cheating. My husband could have reached the moment of penetration and changed his mind, but he didn't. He allowed his desires to trump his commitment to me and our family, so the fallout from his action is a cross he will have to bear. Through prayer and journaling I was able to realize these points:

- There are men out there who do not cheat. I will wait patiently until God sends me one.
- I do not have to adjust my standards and accept his behavior.

- I have a daughter who watches my every move. It is my job to show her how to conduct herself, and to show her what she should not accept.
- My sons are watching as well. I must show them how to respect relationships.
- I must empower my children to communicate effectively and advocate for themselves.

Here are some scriptures regarding temptation, adultery, and the effects of betrayal on your self-esteem:

- Proverbs 6:32 states, "But a man who commits adultery has no sense; whoever does so destroys himself."
- Hebrews 13:4 states, "Let marriage be held in honor among all, and let the marriage bed be undefiled, for God will judge the sexually immoral and adulterous."
- 1 Corinthians 10:13 states, "No temptation has overtaken you except what is common to mankind. And God is faithful; he will not let you be tempted beyond what you can bear. But when you are

tempted, he will also provide a way out so that you can endure it."

- Luke 7:13 states, "When the Lord saw her, his heart went out to her and he said, "Don't cry.""
- Psalm 139:14 states, "I praise you because I am fearfully and wonderfully made; your works are wonderful, I know that full well."

Chapter 3

Don't Ignore the Signs

When you love a man, you learn to accept his flaws. When you are married to that flawed man, you ignore his disturbing behavior. When you have kids with the flawed man that you are married to, you might be tempted to literally stick your head in the sand to avoid seeing his transgressions. I'm not ashamed to admit that I was that woman blinded by love.

Ladies, if it looks like a duck, walks like a duck, and quacks like a duck...it ain't a frog. My husband showed every sign in the book that he was having an affair, and instead of calling it a duck, I pretended it was a frog—and that's how I got burned.

At the advice of family, friends, and various celebrities, I started keeping a journal during my marriage. The primary purpose of keeping the journal was to purge all the negative feelings I'd been storing inside of me. Toxic feelings that slowly ate at my soul like an angry bacterium. But the same way a germ can spread, so does the toxicity of a bad relationship. If not treated, it will attack your mental and physical abilities. Trust me, I know.

I recently revisited my old journal and was astonished to see that twelve years before our divorce was final, I wrote the following sentence: *I think he is cheating*.

When I think back on it all, I wasn't blind, just reluctant to leave him. I had my reasons—which I'll address in another chapter—but just know that I didn't move when I first smelled something fishy. I ignored four key signs.

The first sign that I foolishly ignored was the change in his routine. My husband was a creature of habit just like most men. So, when he started staying out later than he said he would, I noticed immediately. I remember one day when he claimed he was going to a three-hour basketball practice—he was a coach—and didn't return until nine hours later. He didn't appear to have broken a sweat. In fact, he smelt like he'd taken a bath in his favorite cologne.

"How was practice?" I asked.

"Fine," he replied dismissively and made a beeline to the bathroom.

When he came out of the bathroom he crawled into bed and was sleeping before I could get a chance to pepper him with questions.

The second sign that he was cheating reared its head when he started handling his cellphone calls differently. When we first got married, he'd talk on the phone in front of me. There were times when he talked so loudly that I'd have to tell him to go into another room. Then those boisterous phone conversations stopped as fast as water stops flowing when you turn the knob on the sink. He'd get a phone call and instead of talking in front of me, he'd lower his voice and go into the basement. Or, he'd suddenly have something to do away from the home. He'd hop in his car and leave. On top of that, he had a different ring tone. Why would a married man need a different ring tone unless he was trying to differentiate who was calling him?

Did I ever challenge him on his actions? No. I learned very early in my marriage that there are things worth arguing about and things that aren't. I chose to save my suspicions for things that I could prove. I had no way of proving that he was talking to another woman on those phone calls. It was all speculative on my part. When I considered the potential fallout from making a false accusation, I didn't see a worthwhile return on that type of speculative investment.

The third sign was probably the most obvious—our sex life changed. Let me be clear, it was never good to begin with. I spent thirteen years feeling unsatisfied, but I kept trying to encourage him because intimacy is an integral part of any healthy marriage. That physical connection with the person you've sworn your life to is irreplaceable.

On those evenings when he was gone for long stretches of time, I knew that it would be a cold lonely night. After washing up, he'd go straight to bed and be asleep within minutes; his energy zapped like he'd been tased. When my husband no longer wanted to touch me, I knew that he must have been touching someone else. If you asked him today, I'm sure he would argue that I was the one who didn't want sex. Like I said, it wasn't good. I would rather have no sex than bad sex, so there were times I didn't want to, but did.

Which leads me to the fourth sign that he was cheating. There is an old saying: when your mate has less to say to you, it's because he's saying more to someone else. It took me a while to figure it out, but I concluded that the first three signs he was cheating fed off a primary source. They were the *symptoms* of a much deeper *ailment*. My husband's ailment was that he no longer *liked* me—that was the fourth, and arguably most important, sign that he was cheating.

If they were casting for the role of Dr. Jekyll and Mr. Hyde, my ex-husband would have won the job easily. The way he spoke to his coworkers and our friends was opposite of the way he spoke to me at home. Sometimes he spoke to me as if my presence disgusted him. Initially, I chalked it up to him being a little grumpy. But there is a difference between being grumpy and downright mean. When he spoke to me his words were often lathered in vitriol, and no matter how hard I tried to appease him, it was never good enough.

Once, I made the mistake of buying a turkey fryer after he mentioned that he wanted to taste a deep-fried turkey. Since he'd accused me of not listening to him and being in tune with his needs, I thought the gesture would prove that I did pay attention to him. It wasn't until I got to the store and saw the price tag on the fryer that I realized I'd bitten off more than I could chew. Deep fryers—and the accessories like the propane tank—were expensive. I hadn't thought that far ahead. Still, I stupidly bought the deep fryer. I use the word *stupidly* to describe my decision because when I brought it home, he wasn't impressed.

That Thanksgiving was one I'd love to forget. Instead of rejoicing and be thankful for all of God's blessings, it was a miserable day. We hardly spoke to each other. Imagine sitting around the table struggling to come up with things to talk about. Imagine sitting across from the supposed "head of the house" who is doing everything he can to avoid making eye contact with you. Imagine all this happening while your mother sat at the table witnessing it. Imagine being overcome with the feeling that your husband would prefer to be eating Thanksgiving dinner with someone else instead of you.

While I sat there struggling to suppress my hurt long enough to digest the meal that I'd spent all morning preparing, I had a thought: *Other than my kids and mama being healthy, what do I have to be thankful for?*

There was another occasion when we took the kids to an amusement park. After eating and going on various tours within the park, we started playing a game called, Cannon Wars. In this game, you get on opposing sides—roughly ten feet apart—and fire nerf balls at your opponent. One of our kids was on my side and our other child was on his. It was supposed to be all fun. But it didn't take long for me to notice that my husband seemed to be having too much fun. He came after me—and only me—with a level of aggression that seemed out of place. Hunched shoulders. A sinister grimace. Pressed lips. It was like he was lashing out—hitting me without having to use his fist.

When the game was over and we were leaving the game station I thought to myself, *this man really doesn't like me.*

As I've stated before, the truth always comes out. The feeling that my husband didn't like me swirled in my head for years, and then one night it was confirmed. How? He told me to my face. That's right, the man whom I'd been married to for nearly twenty years, at that time, looked me straight in the eyes one day and said, "I don't like you. You need to understand, I don't like you."

I was taken aback more so by the disdain in his voice and the evil that flashed in his eyes, than the fact that he said it. I'd already figured out that he didn't like me. You don't do things with people you don't like. You don't talk to people you don't like. You avoid people you don't like.

I guess I can't be too mad at his confession because it helped me better understand the difference between being tolerated and accepted. Being accepted shows up in more than words. When someone (or a group) accepts you, the confirmation is more in their actions. Being tolerated is just the opposite. You get a steady diet of words, but rarely any actions. Why? Because action requires effort. No one puts effort into something they don't particularly care for.

The "family time" my husband spent with us was for the kids, not me. He and I didn't have any "date" nights. We didn't go to the movies together. On those rare occasions when we did go out to eat dinner—just us adults—it was with a group of people. Never just the two of us.

While watching the movie, *Lady Sings the Blues*, the reality of my situation pierced my soul like an old Billie Holiday tune. All my efforts to salvage my marriage were futile. It was time to let go of the man who didn't like me. Through prayer and journaling I was able to realize this third lesson:

Lesson: 3 ~ Your Gut is God

We're all given the ability to discern. It's often referred to as "women's intuition", but the truth of the matter is, every woman and man can distinguish fake from real. Unfortunately, we don't always use that innate ability. The reasons for our failure to tap into this God given talent varies, but what can't be disputed is that we should use it more. When you stop ignoring God's taps on your shoulder, the drama you repeatedly find yourself in will start to lessen. Like a light bulb that is suddenly turned on in a dark room, all those shadows that you couldn't make out become clear as day. It's like that loud beep a truck makes when it is backing up, even if you don't see the danger, you know it's nearby. Here is what you should do when your spirit starts warning you that something isn't right:

- Listen to your inner voice, the Holy Spirit. Stop moving and find a quiet place where you can pray to God and ask for clarity.

- Keep a journal of dates, times, and episodes of suspicious activity so that if/when you must refer to them, your comments are accurate and detailed.
- Seventy-five percent of all communication is non-verbal. Pay attention to the changes in your spouses' communication patterns. Ask them direct questions and watch their response. Jittery eyes, stuttering, and becoming defensive are signs that your questioning is warranted.
- Hear what is being said, as well as not being said.

Here are some scriptures that address discernment. You can refer to these verses during your time of need:

- Hebrews 4:12 says, "For the word of God is alive and active. Sharper than any double-edged sword, it penetrates even to dividing soul and spirit, joints and marrow; it judges the thoughts and attitudes of the heart."
- Proverbs 1:5 says, "Let the wise listen and add to their learning, and let the discerning get guidance—"

- John 16:13 says, "But when he, the Spirit of truth, comes, he will guide you into all the truth."

Chapter 4

He's Not Worth My Sanity

Depression is real. Anyone who doesn't believe that to be true has lived a very sheltered life. When you step out into this world there will be disappointments that will take you on emotional rollercoasters with more twists and turns than any amusement park ride. Unfortunately, not everyone is emotionally equipped to handle those loops, shimmies, and unexpected drops. I was one of those unequipped people.

At one point during my marriage, I relied on Lexapro to help me manage bouts of depression, but I stopped taking it when my husband expressed concerns about the side effects. After the Andrea Yates case made the news, he concluded that I might "snap" and hurt our kids. I'd never displayed that type of irrational behavior, but he insisted that taking the drug could make me do something dangerous. He had a negative and narrow-minded view of anti-depressants and depression, and it hurt me that he didn't want to understand what depression really looked like. I felt like I was alone in the battle.

To appease my husband, I contacted my doctor and reduced my dosage—wrong move. My sanity was *mine* to manage, not my paranoid husband. No one was going to look out for me better than me. No one knew my emotional state better than me. No one could tell me what helped me better than me. Placing my mate's feelings over my emotional stability is a mistake I'll never make again. His lack of empathy nearly cost me my sanity.

His lack of empathy also showed up in his refusal to apologize for his infidelity. When you're in love you can forgive anything. But when the person you want to forgive makes it clear he couldn't care less about your pain,

10 Things I Learned When My Husband Had a Girlfriend!

reconciliation is not only close to impossible, it is probably not wise.

For someone who *feared* for the life of his children, my husband stayed away from home a lot. I often wondered if he hoped I would do something to our kids so that he could come home and say, "see, I was right, she is crazy!".

One Mother's Day, we'd had a good time at church and a nice dinner with friends afterward. That evening, my husband said he had to go collect some money for a computer he'd worked on. After he left, I laid on the sofa in my robe and watched the movie, *Imitation of Life*.

My eyes were glued to the television, but my mind started to drift. At this point, I had known about the affair and like a 'good little Christian', I decided to forgive and forget. The forgiveness was easy, the forgetting, not so much.

I started thinking about things that I'm embarrassed to admit, but in the interest of transparency, I'll tell you what I thought about that day. I plotted ways to get revenge on my husband and his girlfriend. I thought about killing them both and making it look like an accident. I know, I know, that was rather extreme, but I'm just being honest, it crossed my mind. Fortunately, I was still sane enough to let go of those murderous thoughts. However, I wasn't above devising a scheme to embarrass him.

I considered renting a billboard on the highway and listing both of their names and transgressions. I could go on Facebook and put them both on blast. Those were two options—the first would require me to save some coins, but the second option could be done at no cost and it would only take a few minutes. After a while, those malicious thoughts were snuffed out by my core values. I'm not a killer. I don't live to hurt others. I'm a good person, and good people don't do the bad things I was contemplating.

No matter how much I thought about hurting him, I simply couldn't bring myself to embarrass the man I'd been married to for twenty years. I'd spent our entire marriage protecting his image, I couldn't find it within myself to tear him down. While operation "Embarrass the Hell out of Them" dominated my thoughts, I was suddenly overcome with a feeling of sorrow that sent me whirling. I was crying but no sound escaped my lips. Tears were simply streaming from eyes, down my face, and onto the floor. I could not move nor speak. It was as if I was paralyzed. The tears started to pour from my eyes like Niagara Falls. Before I knew it, I was on the floor crying. I'm talking one of those ugly cries where your face gets distorted, snot seeps you're your nose, your vision gets blurry, and for a moment, you can't hear anything.

While sprawled on the floor, my robe opened and my body was completely exposed. I heard my three-year-old daughter yell from the top of the stairs. "What's wrong, Mama?"

I could hear her sweet voice, but I couldn't look up at her. When I didn't reply she called my son, her older brother. My eight-year-old son has always been extremely protective of me. Naturally, when he saw the condition I was in, he tried to help. He went upstairs and got his SpongeBob bed sheet to cover me. I could only pray they didn't start crying too.

"Here's some tissue, Mama," he said.

"What's wrong with mama?" my daughter asked.

"I think her heart is broken," my son replied.

Let that sink in for a moment. You are at your lowest point and your child—who isn't even old enough to say his multiplication tables without messing up a few times—has the Emotional IQ to know that you are heart broken. The sound of him uttering those words sends chills through my body all these years later.

10 Things I Learned When My Husband Had a Girlfriend!

My kids took turns wiping my face. By the time I could focus, there was a mound of tear-soaked tissue on the floor next to me. That's when it happened. The front door opened and my husband walked in.

"Y'all go upstairs," he barked.

I could hear the pitter-patter of my kid's feet as they ran upstairs. I remained on the floor. My husband stepped over my prone body and walked over to the sofa. He plopped down, sighed, and grabbed the remote control. I could hear the channels changing until he found what he was looking for—the basketball game.

"Trina, you need to get up," was all he said. Nothing more, nothing less.

My daughter appeared at the top of the stairs and shouted, "What you gon' do, Dad?!"

I can laugh about that now because she kept asking him. I remember thinking, "my girl!".

He never answered her question, but he did order her to go back to the bedroom—an order my baby refused to follow.

The next thirty minutes were filled with two sounds: my daughter demanding to know what he was going to do and the voices of the men announcing the basketball game.

10 Things I Learned When My Husband Had a Girlfriend!

My husband watched the basketball game and acted like I was an inanimate object because to acknowledge me there on the floor would force him to face the obvious—I'd found out about his affair.

The more I think about it, his girlfriend—the person who more than likely sent the anonymous letter to me—probably told him she did it. Either way, he knew he was busted. And in true cowardly fashion, he opted to ignore the results of his behavior rather than face the pain he'd caused.

Every Sunday night, my cousins from Birmingham and Virginia would call and we'd talk about topics that ranged from family business to our favorite television shows. True to form, they called that evening to speak to me, but I was in no condition to speak.

"Yeah, she's here, but she can't come to the phone," he said.

They must've asked him why because the next thing that came out of his mouth was, "I don't know. She's here on the floor crying."

Moments later, he walked over and put the phone to my ear. I could hear my cousins shouting my name. I kept opening my mouth, but words wouldn't come out. It's like they were trapped in my throat—one big log jam. Suddenly, everything went blank.

My husband was a former police officer. One of the things he was taught to do to make sure a person was alive was to press his knuckles against the breastplate. If the person doesn't move, the call to 9-1-1 needs to happen immediately. I didn't move. He made the call. When the paramedics arrived, they shoved needles in both of my arms. Those who know me, know that I hate needles. The fact that I didn't have the strength to voice my dislike was an indication of how bad my condition was.

I was transported to a nearby hospital. While in route I remember hearing the paramedics talking about how my heart rate had dropped into the twenties. That's when I got scared and started to panic.

I was only partially coherent while in the Emergency Room and still unable to move or speak. I heard a lot of familiar voices: my mother, a few of my cousins, but the one voice I didn't hear was my husband's. I've seen movies where a patient's body is on the hospital bed but their spirit gets up and leaves. I don't recall seeing a shadowy figure depart my physical frame, but I felt like that's what was happening to me. While the doctors talked and my family members struggled to understand what was happening to me, I was floating around checking out the scene.

"We have run every medical test we can think to run," the Emergency Room physician said, "but we can't find anything medically wrong with her. We think her current state is psychological."

The next thing I knew, I was being transferred to a hospital in Birmingham, Alabama, that had a world-renowned psychiatric ward. I was in a catatonic state. According to my medical records, I was diagnosed with having a "dissociative" episode.

My hospital room ceiling appeared to be decorated in a swirling paisley pattern. I remember this because I stared up at that ceiling for most of the time I was there. The air ducts were dusty and the room reeked of disinfectant. The staff poked at me for days trying to elicit a response. One staff member even placed the tip of her finger inches away from my eye. I guess it was some type of test they do to see if the patient will blink. When I didn't react, they knew I wasn't faking.

I remained in that psychiatric ward for three days. During that three day stay my limbs came alive. My words were no longer trapped in my throat. I became aware of everything happening around me. And most importantly, I could get up and move around.

I couldn't spend all my time in my room because I didn't want them to think that I was being antisocial, so I ventured out into the common area. People from all walks of life were there: an elementary school principal, a doctor, a homeless man, and a slew of other mentally unstable people.

I was asked to join in a game of Scattergories. The homeless man asked to be on my team because he said I looked like I was smart and knew things. Once the game got going and we were calling out answers someone wrote down Samuel Adams for a President for the letter 'A'.

"You mean John Adams?" I said. "Samuel Adams is a beer."

"See, I knew you knew shit!" the homeless man shouted. Scattergories was one of my favorite games. Recreational Therapy was fun. We got to do arts and crafts, and I painted a wooden jewelry box. I painted it purple and gave it to my little girl when I got home.

After the games ended and I returned to my room, I met with my doctor. He told me I had a "dissociative" episode. He explained that my mind would not stop thinking about something, so my body started shutting down. He repeatedly asked what I'd gone through that caused such emotional trauma. I didn't tell him. I simply didn't have the courage to tell him that I was there because I found out my husband had a girlfriend. Through prayer and journaling I was able to realize this fourth lesson:

Lesson: 4 ~ Your Mental Health is Priceless

To all the "church folks" reading this you need to know something...seeking the help of a therapist/counselor will not get you a one-way ticket to hell. I do not believe God would have gifted therapists and counselors with the knowledge they have if He didn't want us to use them. Find a Christian counselor if that makes you feel better, but please see someone.

As far as medication that is often prescribed to stabilize your emotions, I looked at it as a bridge to get me over. People take meds for everything from high blood pressure to infertility; why not mental health. However, I would be remiss to not say that they can have side effects.

The medication made me feel emotionless—zombie-like. For me, that was not healthy.

I had to identify my triggers and address them when I felt an *episode* coming on. My mantra is, and has been for quite a while now, *Great is my peace and my undisturbed composure.*

Before you can take care of anyone else you must make sure your mental stability is intact. I was so wrapped up in my pain that I had an emotional breakdown. I'm not suggesting that you will react the same way that I did if you should experience a similar personal crisis, but I am saying that you should do the following things as they pertain to your mental health:

- Do not be afraid to go to counseling when you know that you are feeling anxiety about personal matters.
- When you pray to God make sure your mental stability is included in your prayers.
- When your kids witness your emotional breakdown, it can affect them in ways that don't show. Make sure you get them someone to talk to.

Here are some scriptures that address emotional stability. You can refer to these verses during your time of need:

- Philippians 4:6-7 states, "Do not be anxious about anything, but in every situation, by prayer and petition, with thanksgiving, present your requests to God. And the peace of God, which transcends all understanding, will guard your hearts and your minds in Christ Jesus."
- Philippians 1:9-10 states, "And it is my prayer that your love may abound and more, with knowledge and all discernment, so that you may approve what is excellent, and so be pure and blameless for the day of Christ."
- Psalm 3:3 states, "But you, Lord, are a shield around me, my glory, the One who lifts my head high."
- 2 Timothy 1:7 states, "For God has not given us the spirit of fear; but of power, and of love, and of a **sound mind**."
- Proverbs 3:5-6 states, "Trust in the Lord with all your heart, and do not lean on your own understanding. In all your ways acknowledge him, and he will make straight your paths."

- Ephesians 5:6-10 states, "Let no one deceive you with empty words, for because of these things the wrath of God comes upon the sons of disobedience. Therefore, do not become partners with them; for at one time you were darkness, but now you are light in the Lord. Walk as children of light (for the fruit of light is found in all that id good and right and true), and try to discern what is pleasing to the Lord.

Chapter 5

I Must Own My Flaws

Transparency is key if a true breakthrough is going to happen. I learned that in counseling and it's something I had to face head on. Why do I bring up the word, transparency? Because for me to offer credible advice, I must be willing to admit my own wrongs.

Back in 2000, when AOL had a chat room called, Black Voices, I engaged in a raunchy chat with a man. The back and forth flirting lasted a few weeks.

10 Things I Learned When My Husband Had a Girlfriend!

Although I never met the man and nothing came of it, I was guilty of engaging in an emotional affair.

My husband learned about the emotional affair and printed the chat. He took the transcript to our pastors. I assume his intent was to humiliate me. Or, maybe it was to lay the groundwork for a divorce. However, the only feedback he received from the pastor and the other male members of the church that he discussed the situation with was to give me what I wanted. Even though he attempted to bring shame upon me by divulging our personal business, it was obvious that the discovery hurt him. And as well all know, hurt people…hurt people.

I can admit that I was wrong. I own it. Regardless of how unhappy I was in our marriage, no one put a gun to my head and made me entertain that other man. To this day, he still thinks I met the man when I went to my cousin's wedding. I have told him a thousand times, considering how sexually frustrated and miserable I was, nothing would give me greater pleasure than to say, "Yes, I slept with someone else and it was freaking amazing", but I can't say that because it is not true.

I would have loved for him to have to live with the knowledge that another man physically satisfied his wife in ways he could not. The fact of the matter is, no other man touched me during the twenty-four plus years that we were married. Truth be told, I didn't even touch myself during those long years of sexual unfulfillment. I don't have any regrets because my relationship with God means the world to me. I would not have been able to live with myself if I had crossed that line.

As much as I cringe when I think back at some of the trauma I endured and sometimes wonder if I should've taken advantage of opportunities when I could have been selfish, I'm happy that I handled things the way I did. The main reason why I'm happy is because I can now look directly into my children's eyes and feel no shame.

Your child—especially a daughter—is programmed to have a soft spot for their father. We all know of situations when *daddy* can walk on water and *mama* can't do anything right. Even the late rapper Tupac Shakur once said in his song, Dear Mama: *'Even though we had different daddies; the same drama, when things went wrong, we blamed mama.'*

Sometimes women are asked to carry the load and the blame, but trust me when I tell you, those kids will grow up and learn the truth. They will figure out that on those nights when they were able to go back and get a second helping of dinner it was because *mama* chose not to eat. They will figure out that the reason the lights stayed on in the house is because *mama* passed on buying a new dress or shoes for work. They will one day understand that their *mama* took a second job that stretched her workdays to sixteen hours so that they could have new tennis shoes on the first day of school.

Yes, I may have erred in judgment, but the reason why I can write about it today is because I know that if you want to be heard and respected, you must acknowledge and own your transgressions. So, don't be afraid to be transparent with the people you care for and whom you want to respect you. When the dust settles, they will respect the fact that you owned your flaws. At that point, you can walk and talk with your head high, your voice unwavering, and the confidence in knowing that the respect you receive has been earned. Through prayer and journaling I was able to realize this fifth lesson:

Lesson: 5~ Be Transparent

Holding a grudge is exhausting. It requires thought, effort, and it drains your emotional battery the way a light that's left on inside of your car can drain your car's battery. Often, to avoid this battery draining experience, most people will either pretend the transgression didn't occur or walk away from a relationship.

Walking away from a relationship is easy if you don't have any personal or professional ties to the person, but what if you do? How do you move past an incident that is unresolved—just act like it didn't happen? You can't. It's impossible. Every time you see that person, your thoughts loop and it becomes Groundhog Day. The details of the incident come back and scroll across your mind like an old movie.

Now, I want you to close your eyes and envision that you are the person who caused the relationship turmoil. You are the person that has done something that causes another person to roll their eyes at the mention of your name or become nauseous at the sight of you. Imagine yourself being cast as the antagonist. Imagine your parents being ashamed of you, your friends avoiding you, and even worse, the person children grow to hate. Doesn't feel good, huh? The thought of that level ostracism makes you want to find a corner and curl up in the fetal position, huh?

10 Things I Learned When My Husband Had a Girlfriend!

Well, I'm here to tell you that you can avoid becoming a pariah in your family's eyes by doing one simple thing after you make a mistake that hurts someone you love—own it. Don't partially own it. Don't throw other people under the bus while you explain your side. Your confession shouldn't be littered with conjunctions: "but", "however", and "so". That's the cowards' approach to confessions and no one—especially your kids—respects a coward. To truly "own" your mistake only requires a few things: eye contact, sincerity, and acknowledgment of the wrongdoing that is devoid of any excuses…a simple, *'I was wrong for what I did. I have no excuses. I'm sorry. Please forgive me.'*

Transparency will take you down roads a lie can't travel. Ask God for forgiveness of your sins and then ask God to give you the words and humility to explain your transgressions to the people who need to hear your apology. God will pave the bumpy road you have to travel.

Here are some scriptures that address honesty and humility. You can refer to these verses during your time of need:

- Proverbs 11:3 states, "The integrity of the upright guides them, but the unfaithful are destroyed by their duplicity."
- Proverbs 21:3 states, "To do what is right and just is more acceptable to the Lord that sacrifice."
- 1 John 1:6 states, "If we claim to have fellowship with him and yet walk in the darkness, we lie and do not live out the truth."

Chapter 6

I'm Stronger Than I Thought

A friend once told me that procrastination is fear in disguise. The thought of failure paralyzes us to the point that not acting on what our gut is telling us to do seems like a safer route. But it's not. In fact, not acting is in some ways worse than acting and making a choice that doesn't yield the desired results. There are lessons to be learned even in failure, and if you don't act, you lose the opportunity to both succeed and learn.

Now that I've grown as a person, I realize that my reluctance to leave—although my female intuition told me that I should—was a form of fear. Let me be clear, I'm acknowledging that I was scared, but I'm not beating myself up over being scared. I had a right to be scared. The decision of whether to leave hinged on more than just my feelings. I had to think about how my actions would affect my kids. Would they hate me? Would they prefer to live with him? Would their grades take a turn for the worse? Would they need counseling? If they needed counseling, how would I pay for it? Those are some of the real questions that cross your mind when you decide to leave a marriage.

I also believed and prayed that God would heal our marriage; that the affair—and how we got past it—would be a testimony that we could one day use to inspire other couples in marriage ministry. I prayed that God would make me the wife he wanted me to be. I know that I serve a "late in the midnight hour".

One day, I heard a teaching about free will and God not overriding our will. That's the beauty of God, we are His creation, but rather than force us to love and serve Him, He gives us the choice to do so. My husband had a choice and he made it. According to him, everything was my fault. Let him tell it, if I hadn't done immoral things (like the sexual conversations with the man) and been a better wife, he wouldn't have behaved the way he did.

While washing dishes and talking to God about the duties of a husband and why mine found it so difficult to be with me, God spoke to my spirit. I heard Him say: *You're asking him to do something he can't do.*

I continued to stand there washing dishes and moments later God told me: *Your earthly husband is going to be who he is. You should continue living right. I will protect you.*

I mumbled, "He gets the same *Word* I get. He goes to men's conferences just like I go to women's conferences. We both know what it takes to maintain a healthy marriage and the ways trouble can rear its head."

It was at that moment that I acknowledged and accepted that I was the only one rowing in the relationship. It should not have been a surprise that our boat was drifting sideways. Through prayer and journaling I was able to realize this sixth lesson:

Lesson: 6 ~ Don't be Afraid to Leap

Fear is not of God. I'll say that again...fear is not of God. Your gut is God. And when your gut is telling you it's time to move on, it is in fact, God telling you to move on. Since God is not in the business of letting his children fall flat on their faces, He is encouraging you to take the necessary steps toward sanity and happiness knowing that He will be there to catch you if you stumble.

While you are debating whether to walk away from a toxic marriage, I want you to also consider how staying is impacting your children. I have a daughter whom I want to understand how a loving relationship should look. I want her to be able to spot a man with the ability to treat her like the queen that I've always told her she was. I have boys who need to know how to treat their wives. Seeing their mother cry and their father act like he doesn't care, is not the type of example that will help my sons become the men they need to be.

When you choose to stay in a marriage that sets the wrong example for your children, you become implicit should they grow up to become the toxic person in their future relationship. That may sound harsh, but it's the truth. You are either contributing to your child's growth or you are contributing to stunting their growth. Which kind of contributor do you want to be?

Here are some scriptures that address strength during a storm:

- Isiah 41:10 states, "So do not fear, for I am with you; do not be dismayed, for I am your God. I will strengthen you and help you; I will uphold you with my righteous hand."
- 2 Thessalonians 3:3 states, "But the Lord is faithful, and he will strengthen you and protect you from the evil one."
- 2 Timothy 1:7 states, "For the Spirit God gave us does not make us timid, but gives us power, love and discipline."

Chapter 7

He Cheated, I Changed

The longer my husband and I stayed together after the truth about his affair came out, I noticed a couple of things happening to me. First, I became more aggressive toward him. Every time I looked at him, I felt like I was about to snap. He would call me "hateful" and "spiteful" and "irrational", but he had no idea that there were times when I was angry enough to become deadly.

10 Things I Learned When My Husband Had a Girlfriend!

I would say mean things because words were my weapon. Anyone who knows me, knows that I'm not normally that type of person. But the anger grew inside of me like steam in a teapot. It had to be released somehow.

The second thing I noticed is that I became resentful toward God. I could not understand why my Lord and Savior would subject me to so much pain. It simply did not make sense to me.

Because I could feel my attitude changing for the worse, I decided to move out of our house and get an apartment. Unfortunately, because we were in bankruptcy during that time period, I couldn't qualify for a sizable loan. I was trapped. I would pace back and forth in our house like a tiger seeking an opportunity to break free from its cage.

At one point, I even wondered if not being able to get an apartment was God's way of forcing me to stay, so that my husband and I could possibly work things out. But the longer I stayed, the worse our communication became. From my perspective, God let me down and I was bitter as hell.

With nowhere to turn, I reached out to the ordained ladies at my church. They scheduled a meeting and we sat down to talk. Truth be told, they mainly listened while I vented about my husband and my frustration with God. Why was God forcing me to stay in a terrible marriage? Why was God allowing the situation to get worse? The questions spewed from my mouth like vomit while tears poured from my eyes like a river.

After close to an hour of purging all my anger, I felt relieved. It was as if a weight had been lifted off my shoulders. By the end of the evening all I wanted to do was ask God for forgiveness and praise Him.

I re-entered my home with a new attitude. I was a single "married" woman. I became more independent and took ownership of the finances, discipline, and even house repairs. Through prayer and journaling I was able to realize this seventh lesson:

Lesson: 7~ Control What You Can

God will not override anyone's will. Your spouse must own his role in the erosion of your marriage and want to change his behavior. In my case, my husband refused to own his shortcomings. So, I stopped worrying about his actions and adjusted my prayers. That shift in focus freed me emotionally and elevated my faith.

10 Things I Learned When My Husband Had a Girlfriend!

I'm not going to lie; it took some time for me to master the attitude shift I needed to undergo to break the habit of wanting him to change. It was behavior that I'd perfected over twenty years. To think that I would be able to do a one hundred-eighty degree turn overnight was unrealistic. I'm telling you this because you need to know that there will be moments when you will want to go to your default—hoping he'll change. I'm telling you now, that is an exercise in futility. Focus on your own transformation and let God handle the rest.

Here are some scriptures that address transformation:

- Romans 12:2 states, "Do not conform to the pattern of this world, but be transformed by the renewing of your mind. Then you will be able to test and approve what God's will is—his good, pleasing and perfect will."
- Colossians 3:9-10 states, "Do not lie to each other, since you have taken off your old self with its practices and have put on the new self, which is being renewed in knowledge in the image of its Creator."
- 2 Corinthians 3:18 states, "And we all, who with unveiled faces contemplate the Lord's glory, are being

transformed into his image with ever-increasing glory, which comes from the Lord, who is the Spirit."

Chapter 8

I Was Enough

There is nothing more sobering than the realization that sometimes the people you work hardest to please will never be satisfied with your efforts. This isn't a mind-blowing revelation if you're applying it to the workforce. Having to work for a boss who is determined to minimize your accomplishments while highlighting your mistakes, is as old as the sands in the widest desert. However, when this realization shows up within your marriage it can hit you harder than a punch from Mike Tyson.

    I came face to face with this reality during my marriage. No matter how hard I tried to cater to my husband, he was never satisfied. In hindsight, I realize that his negativity was the first sign he'd emotionally checked out. But when you are committed to making things work, failure to see the obvious becomes as commonplace as breathing.

    A classic example of my inability to please the narcissist I was married to came on the night of his fiftieth birthday in 2015. My ex-husband's dream car was a Corvette. Why? Who knows; it could have been an indicator that he was going through some sort of mid-life crisis. Maybe he liked the way the car looked: the aerodynamic body, the eight cylinders that made the engine roar, or the way heads turned whenever the car appeared on any scene. I never asked him what his motivation was for being fixated on getting a Corvette because I didn't care. The price tag was nowhere close to what we could afford, so delving deeper into the *why* was futile.

    Since purchasing a sports car was out of the question, my kids and I decided to do something for him that we

10 Things I Learned When My Husband Had a Girlfriend!

thought would be less expensive and much more meaningful—we threw him a surprise birthday party. After all, he'd never had one and it would be an opportunity for his family and friends to come and celebrate with him. He'd be the star of the show. I figured that would be enough to assuage his narcissism, but I have never been more wrong.

The party was held at a sports bar so that his college friends and family members could really enjoy themselves. I took out a pay day loan to pay for this elaborate party. Yes, I know what you're thinking—bad move. But hey, I was desperate to please him and I really thought this would be a night he'd never forget.

The party went off without a hitch. All the guests seemed to have a good time. There was laughter, dancing, gifts, and some people even penned money on him. Outside of the birth of our kids, it was one of those times when I felt he appreciated something I did for him.

After the party ended and we all went home, he summoned my kids and I into the family room. We were expecting him to thank us for the wonderful evening, but we received resembled more of a basketball coach scolding his players for a lack of hustle.

He told us that the party was great, but he felt we should show him that same level of appreciation year-round. The lecture became a referendum on all the things we didn't do for him and how he felt we should all work harder to worship the ground he walked on.

The kids were baffled. I was baffled. He told us we didn't love, appreciate, or respect him, and then gave, what he thought, were cogent examples. He complained about not having a plate of food for him after basketball practice. Of course, he didn't care to hear about the times when I forfeited my meal so that there would be enough for the kids to get seconds when they were hungrier than usual. He made a big stink about the kids sitting in *his* recliner and not getting out of his chair whenever he came home from work. Like a politician who is disinterested in answering a tough question, he sidestepped the fact that I suggested he put in the basement in his mancave. He left the recliner in the living room and never bothered to bring it to the basement, so the kids did what kids do—they sat on it.

It angers me to think back on that night. His words stung me, but I'm an adult so I could take it. What causes me the most pain upon reflection is the way his lecture crushed my kids. They appeared flabbergasted. I felt helpless and sick to my stomach.

His behavior that evening, and the emotional impact it had on my kids, was like a tough grass stain on the knees of a pair of blue jeans; no matter how hard you soak and scrub the stain, you'll never completely get it out. My kids were never the same after that evening. Sure, they still loved their father, but the adoration that twinkled in their eyes whenever he entered a room faded.

That incident was the straw that broke the camel's back for me. I fasted and prayed for thirty days after that evening, waiting for God to remove my desire to get a divorce. But, at the end of my fasting season, I still had the same peace. With more confidence than I can ever remember having, I told him I wanted to leave. He told me that if leaving will make me happy then that was what I should do—so I left.

Through prayer and journaling I was able to realize the eight lesson:

Lesson: 8 ~ Don't Beat Yourself Up

It is so easy to lose yourself in your marriage. It's also easy to lose yourself in the happiness of your kids. However, I want you to know that it is just as easy to invest in your own happiness. You must be brave enough to put your mental and spiritual health first. If you aren't feeling right, your efforts to make other people happy won't go right.

The first step to putting yourself first is to stop beating yourself up and recognize that if you are doing everything that you know is right, then you are doing enough. Seek therapy if you need to. Seek the counsel of an elder whom you respect. Spend some alone time with yourself; reconnect with the things that you like. Do whatever you need to do to rebuild your self-esteem when you don't have a partner with the skills—or desire—to help you.

Here are some scriptures that address your value:

- Proverbs 31:10 states, "A wife of noble character who can find? She is worth far more than rubies."
- Exodus 19:5 states, "Now if you obey me fully and keep my covenant, then out of all nations you will be

my treasured possession. Although the whole earth is mine."

- Isaiah 43:4 states, "Since you are precious and honored in my sight, and because I love you, I will give people in exchange for you, nations in exchange for your life."

Chapter 9

Finding Peace and Keeping It

After I left my husband; I went through a period where I didn't cry. In fact, I showed little emotion. Many of my friends and family members told me that I was going through some form of shock. A few even stared at me in ways that made me uncomfortable; like I was an inmate on suicide watch. It seemed like the more I told them I was doing fine, the more they questioned my mental state. Considering the "dissociative" episode I had years earlier, I guess their reaction was understandable.

I ignored most of their piercing gazes and side-eye looks. Handling my responsibilities as a mother and getting my life together were at the top of my priority list. Trying to convince the world that I didn't need to be in a stray jacket was a burden I was already too tired to carry.

You can blot out the white noise that surrounds you and become engrossed in your everyday tasks, but that doesn't mean you don't hear the things that are being said to you and about you. I heard the concern in the voices of those who loved me, and I knew that their queries came from a place of caring and concern. Instead of getting angry, I assured my support network that I heard and recognized their concerns and that I would be fine.

I had a long conversation with my pastor. I explained to him that I hadn't cried once since leaving my husband. I told him how concerned my friends and family members were about my mental state, and I asked him if he thought something was wrong with me because I wasn't sad.

"How long were you married?" he asked.

"Twenty-five years," I replied.

"And you've been unhappy and sad in that marriage for years...am I right?"

"Yes," I said, unsure where he was going with his questioning.

"Don't you see, Katrina…you've been mourning the loss of your marriage for years. You've already cried all your tears. That's why you don't have any tears right now."

His words illuminated all that was emotionally dark for me up until that point. The reason I didn't cry after we broke up was because I was already all cried out. I now know that the praying and fasting that I'd done led me to a place I'd often heard about, but had never had the privilege of visiting—perfect peace.

Through prayer and journaling I was able to realize this ninth lesson:

Lesson: 9~ Pray and Fast

In order to hear God's instructions, you must remove all the white noise around you. You must create or find a quiet place; some place where you can be still and hear. To facilitate the hearing of God's word, I highly recommend you pray and fast.

It is through fasting and prayer that I was able to stay in the Word and fully embrace the reality that you can't change people, situations, and circumstances. And because the Bible instructs us to fast in private, I never broadcasted what I was doing to my family; a decision that I know contributed to their concern about my emotional state.

All you can do is work on you and be present for that moment when God sends a person or thing your way that signals your new journey has begun.

Another thing that is important for you to understand so that you won't fall back into bad habits of making moves prior to God's guidance and trying to tackle battles that are not yours, is that your mental and physical health should become a top priority. Your ability to minister to others is undermined if the people you are ministering to have questions about your own faculties.

Here are some scriptures that address fasting that I believe can help you:

- Ezra 8:23 states, "So we fasted and petitioned our God about this, and he answered our prayers."
- Matthew 6:17-18 states, "But when you fast, put oil on your head and wash your face, so that it will not be

obvious to others that you are fasting, but only to your Father, who is unseen' and your Father, who sees what is done in secret, will reward you."

- Matthew 6:16 states, "When you fast, do not look somber as the hypocrites do, for they disfigure their faces to show others they are fasting. Truly I tell you, they have received their reward in full."

Chapter 10

I Will Survive

I have been singing karaoke for over twenty-five years and I absolutely love it. Can I sing? Not at all, but that doesn't stop me from going every time I get a chance. I will do karaoke any and everywhere, from a cruise ship to the local karaoke spot to the Cat's Meow in both New Orleans and Las Vegas. When I first started, Gloria Gaynor's "I Will Survive" was my go-to karaoke jam. I didn't have a routine or anything, but I was quite entertaining, which is what I think the audience loves about me when I sing. Little did I know that song would become one of many soundtracks of my life. I remember my sister-in-law saying to me, 'You know that's your testimony, right?' That was back in the early 2000's and she was right.

It was not that I thought I couldn't live without him, but I didn't want to embarrass him by leaving him. Funny, right? The affair and the woman embarrassed me, yet I was still considerate of not making him look bad by leaving him. Oh, the irony. He certainly wasn't concerned with embarrassing me. I even thought about committing suicide and making it look like an accident so that he wouldn't have to live with the shame of his wife killing herself to get away from him. I shake my head at myself now for being so weak.

So, trust me when I tell you, you are stronger than you give yourself credit for. The God that lives on the inside of you is bigger than ANY problem you face and any devil that tries to come against you. Proverbs 10:22 tells us blessings from God make us rich and He doesn't add sorrow with it. Marriage was not designed to be sorrowful on the part of either spouse. Communicating your needs is equally important as meeting the needs of your spouse.

10 Things I Learned When My Husband Had a Girlfriend!

When two people love each other and have their hearts and minds set on making the best life possible for themselves, that's personal growth. When they grow along with their spouse, that's relationship growth, and doing those things together can make marriage a wonderful thing. A marriage full of prayer, joy, open communication, laughter, intimacy, understanding, financial peace, and growth, among other things, is real relationship goals.

However, that is not always the case. I'm not advocating divorce, NOT AT ALL. I am all for if you can work it out, by any means please do. However, both people must be on the same page. Both spouses have to be committed to doing what they need to do as individuals and as a couple to make the marriage work; to make the marriage grow; to help the marriage heal, and to move on from whatever infidelity has transpired. However, if you find yourself in a place like I did, where moving on is not possible and divorce is your only option, then you too will survive. Get the counseling and the healing you need so you can make the next chapter of your life the best chapter of your life. We are supposed to live life abundantly, to the fullest. Getting a divorce does not change that.

Lesson 10 ~ Life Goes on and You Are Not Forgotten

These final scriptures will assure you that you are not alone:

- Deuteronomy 31:6 says, "Do not be afraid or terrified because of them, for the Lord your God goes with you; he will never leave you nor forsake you."
- 2 Corinthians 4:8-9 says, "We are hard pressed on every side, but not crushed; perplexed, but not in despair; persecuted, but not abandoned; struck down, but not destroyed."
- Exodus 14:14 tells us, "The LORD will fight for you, and you shall hold your peace."

Epilogue

I've been divorced since November of 2016. Since that time, I have changed jobs once, filed for bankruptcy, obtained a second master's degree (which I paid for out-of-pocket), and published this book. It has not been an easy road. I am down to one income and I am working to become financially secure by investing and building my savings and emergency fund.

My ex-husband and I share custody of the two youngest children, and just like divorce is new, so is trying to co-parent. It has been a true learning experience, and even

10 Things I Learned When My Husband Had a Girlfriend!

when you think you're getting the hang of it, something unexpected will happen to remind you that you aren't.

I scoured the internet for resources on divorce, life after divorce, and co-parenting, but I didn't find anything that aligned with my beliefs and preferences; which is why I've decided to launch my own podcast, so stay tuned.

I am looking forward to the next door that God will open and where it will lead me. I refuse to believe that nearly twenty-five years of marriage was a waste. I will not let that be my story. My story will be one of healing, hope, and restoration for myself and others.

I was once asked if I felt I took an "L". After reading my story I know some people will feel I did, but I don't feel that way. My motto is, "Never a loss. Always a LESSON." There is a lesson in everything we experience. You just have to be willing to recognize it and learn from it. Remember, nothing catches God by surprise. You live and you learn, and Lord knows I've learned a lot. Now, I'm about to start living.

KT